TO MY ONE &

THANK YOU SO MUCH FOR ALL
YOUR HELP WITH EDITING & SUPPORT
THROUGH THIS PROCESS, I DON'T
THINK I WOULD HAVE BEEN AS
CONFIDENT ABOUT THE END
PRODUCT AS I AM WITHOUT YOUR
LOVE & ENCOURAGEMENT!

I HOPE YOU ENJOY READING
IT AGAIN & AGAIN BECAUSE
I KNOW YOU WILL!

Love
Belle
XOXOXO
Kris

MY JOURNEY FROM BEATINGS TO BEAUTY

My Journey from Beatings to Beauty

Belle

Rev. date: 10/11/2017

To order additional copies of this book, contact:
Xlibris
1-888-795-4274
www.Xlibris.com
Orders@Xlibris.com
753713

Contents

I wrote this book for and dedicate it to any woman who was or is being abused. I hope it helps you to see there is a life beyond abuse and a way out.

I also dedicate it to my two beautiful children who were and are my strength as well as my reason to keep on living life to find the peace and beauty in it.

Prologue

Since I was a teenager writing has been my way of dealing with life and all it has thrown at me. It took me twenty-two years to write eighty-three poems that I felt were good enough to include in this book. Now that I am finished writing the poems, I am back at the beginning again, reading all that I have created. I take my readers on my journey down memory lane as I write about all the feelings, inspirations and what I have learned along the way. My road of life was pretty rough at times but, I feel this book is something that some or maybe even many can relate to and hopefully be empowered by my love for my family and life in general. No matter how big the mountains we must climb, if we stay positive and believe in ourselves we can do anything.

The beginning

Have you ever felt like "Why me? Why can't life just be easier for me?" I have worked so hard to get here. I left home on my 16th Birthday and never looked back, there was more love out there than I would ever find at home. I have never had an easy go, I worked my ass off for everything I have as well as who I am today. For the first time in my life I can finally say "I love me!" I love who I am and the job I have done raising my two beautiful children. I truly love and appreciate life. It's not like I am rich (far from it) and it's not like I am stuck up or think I am perfect. I am just so happy right here where I am right now. I have always looked for the silver lining around every cloud and when life got rough I wrote about it. Sometimes rambling like this and sometimes I wrote poems however, those always took extreme emotions or a few glasses of savignon blanc. I wrote to express my feelings, to process all I was going through, especially the stuff I should keep to myself because if I said it out loud certain people wouldn't appreciate the truth. Definitely not when it comes from a teenage girl. When I started writing it was on scraps of paper that always got lost until I came back to Powell River from Alberta. When I had just turned eighteen, I was soul searching after my first adventure so far away from home. I had just dumped my free loader boyfriend and I was trying to find myself. I bought a lined exercise book, strapped on my roller blades and started looking for myself.... I didn't really know what I was looking for but looking inside was too painful so I chose to look outward. Powell River is a beautiful

1

little city on the Sunshine Coast of British Columbia. There is an ocean view from almost anywhere in town and the people all know each other. The most amazing place to raise a family or just be a kid. So how did I get here? Right now, writing this book, that I am in the process of getting published. Well, about eight years ago I entered a poetry contest with the international library of poetry. The same poem I entered six years before that, except I had words such as, like, and, but, as well as other words that don't belong at the beginning of a sentence. I took them out and entered the contest a second time with the same poem. To my disbelief I won. The International Library of Poetry asked me if they could publish my poem in a book with many other poets. This is that Poem...

Leaving me

You left a whisper in my ear,
I'll never hear it dance off your lips again.
I dread to see you with great fear,
My sadness might bring back the rain.
You left your sweetness on my tongue,
That I wish would go away.
In your head rings songs I sung,
I hope they haunt you every day.
In my mind you are a child,
In my heart you are a man.
In my bed you stayed a while,
I'll try not to hate you if I can.
So as always I carry on,
I hope you don't forget.
The pain you gave me makes me strong,
One day leaving me, you will regret.

Disbelief

Naturally I said "Yes!" The book was called "Collected Whispers" and it was such a beautiful book filled with many talented poets. It didn't take long after that book was published before I started to hear from all different publishers. However, I was not happy with what any of them offered so I looked into self publishing and that is when I found XLibris. I was very impressed with them so I started saving my money. Now I am finally here I really hope you, the reader, enjoy this book of poems and other tales. I felt just a bunch of poems wasn't enough, I wanted to tell a little about my life and what made me write them in the first place. So let's start with a few poems that need no explanation.

The poem

Once I put my pen to the paper
I can take you anywhere
I can take you to a mountain
And make you feel the intense rush of climbing to the top
I can put you in my arms in the midst
Of the most hot passionate kiss but,
You do not taste the sweetness of my lips
I find to release an emotion
It flows more freely from a pen
And ends up as meaningful words on my page
But, when the pen is removed from the paper
And the book is closed
All of a sudden you stop
Wait
Realize
It was just a poem

Lucky charm

If I hung a lucky charm around my neck
Would my luck change?
Or would it stay the same tomorrow
As it was today
If I hang it right side up
I will collect all good luck
If I hang it upside down
I'll spread my luck all over town
I hope if good luck comes
It won't go away
I will save it in my pocket
For a rainy day

Fairies

Can you hear them?
I can, the whispering of
Their velvety wings beating
The air as they dance
Like snowflakes fluttering
And falling, glittering like
Diamonds in the sky
The most mysteriously magical
Creature in the world of fantasy
Sprinkling dust and casting spells
To bloom flowers and make
Babies dream
Fairies are so splendidly
Busy on beautiful crisp
Spring mornings

Embarrassment

Some of my poems come with a back story so you understand how I felt or why I wrote them, for example, "Ode to men", I had this buddy that had been my close friend since kindergarten. He had recently gotten a job in the forest industry shortly after graduation and he now had a nice big truck and lots of money in his pocket. He asked me if I wanted to go to a party with him in Wildwood which was a 20 minute drive from where I lived at the time. I was more than happy to go with him since we were such good friends and I trusted him like a brother. He picked me up from my house in his great big truck and we went for a 4x4 before the party. Once we got to the party he gave me a few beers, invited me into a room and offered me some cocaine. When I said "No thank you" he seemed a little offended but got over it quickly. We hung out at the party for another hour and a half. While we were having a smoke on the back deck he made a pass at me, leaning in for a kiss and a squeeze. I didn't want to ruin our lifelong friendship by complicating it with sex. When I explained that to him, he blew a fit, kicked a couple planters over on the deck, called me a "Cock tease" and jumped in his truck, peeled out and drove away. Leaving me stranded and embarrassed so I left on foot and in tears. I had to walk for over 2 hours in the rain to get home. Once I got back to my house and into dry p.j.'s, I sat down and wrote "Ode to men" in less than 5 minutes….. So here it is….

Ode to men

I can't say I'm old and wise
Yet I know what I'm saying when it comes to guys
They think they're all that with their trucks and their drugs
So us women consider them idiotic thugs
They show they have balls with big tires and an engine that roars
So they can go to the bar, get drunk and pick up whores
Us smart women know where it's at
We're sick of their lies, bullshit and skack
We don't want men with attitudes and wheels
Only looking for ways to cop cheap feels
So take your shit called charm and shove it up your ass
So we can do what we want and smoke lots of grass
To come to our closing we don't give a fuck
And personally think that all men suck

Observation

When I was eighteen years old and trying to find myself I used to spend a lot of time at a local coffee shop called the "Java Jungle", owned by a friend of mine. Across the street was a place they called the dive shop. It was well known that drugs were sold and done there. I wrote this poem from what I saw sitting in the coffee shop window watching the people that came and went from there. Even though I had no clue about addiction at that time in my life I had never tried or knew someone close enough to me that tried drugs like that. It was interesting to see my perspective as a kid, still pretty innocent and trusting. Although, I actually had a pretty good idea, despite my lack of experience. "Reality" and "Irony" have no drug or addiction influence on them. They are how I felt dealing with being a kid on my own with the responsibilities of an adult.

Addict

He lurks in his corner
Hiding in the shadows
From what?
Who knows?
Maybe himself
Unable to deal with reality
Using his drug to escape
From what?
Only he could tell you
If he had a clue himself
It's sad
Makes you think
What could have happened
Or gone wrong?
To make him only exist
Not live

Reality

Everyone wants a fairytale life but,
How many people have one?
Reality is rainy days, broken windows and bills.
Everyone walks down the road of life,
Sometimes our paths cross with others then stray off again.
The road may be smooth, straight and flat or
windy with roots and rocks sticking out,
Either way if we are strong we will keep on going.
Of course!
Survival of the fittest!

Irony

Irony is a major part of life,
Maybe just a major part of my life.
Destiny can be changed,
Irony comes and goes as it pleases.
In my life irony works in evil ways,
So once I get my head above water,
The tide comes in and I'm drowning again.
I don't understand why it works the way it does,
Cause if I did,
I'd change it.
But, then it wouldn't be irony.

Self-discovery

I spent a lot of time roller blading around this gorgeous town (city) of mine writing, finding myself. No matter how much I struggled with my feelings from my past, my loveless childhood I found comfort in my writing. I found a euphoric state, a release of what was hurting me, what was dragging me under. No matter how hard I tried I could not get my mother to love me for me. To except who I was or even who I came from despite the fact she chose the man she had me with. My soul purpose in life was to try to please her to find a way to make her love me no matter how hopeless my feat was I gave all I had. So these next few poems express my frustration and loneliness…

Frustrated

As I wade among many mixed thoughts and emotions,
I pause,
Trying with all my strength to decide where?
Or how?
To stand amongst the many views.
Which road to take?
Knowledge?
Experience?
Pleasure?
Or love?
I guess only time will tell.
You hold your own destiny in your hand, and if
you follow your heart and your conscience,
The road will come to you.
Remember the road may not always be easy
and if you try hard and never give up,
It will take you to the top!

Alone

A lot of people don't know
What it's like to be alone
Really alone
It is so empty and unexplainable
Like waves crashing on the shore
On a quiet night
They seem to sound so distant
Distant from everyone and everything
That is how I feel
It's not like someone who's in distress
Who always has someone to turn to?
To lean on
Could ever even imagine
What it could be like
To climb a mountain of despair all by themselves

Just me

Why am I so empty
I need to feel loved
But no one wants to
I long to be held
I want someone to need me
To want me there
To hold and comfort them
But no one wants to
Could you please listen
Hear what I need to say
Feel my pain and my pleasure
But no one wants to
Kiss me gently, hold my hand
Whisper softly, understand me
But no one wants to
Except me

Despair

I had a friend that had a baby really young and still wanted to be a kid once in a while so I would take the little guy overnight and babysit him so my friend could have a break. I loved the little guy so it was never a problem. One night she asked me but I had an exam at the college the next morning so I couldn't take him. When I got home after my exam my phone was ringing off the hook. I kind of had a feeling in the pit of my stomach. I answered the phone and I couldn't understand what she was saying she was crying so hard. Once I finally calmed her down enough to understand what she was saying I couldn't believe my ears. That poor young girl had lost her beautiful son to sudden infant death syndrome. I tried to comfort her as I fell to the floor trying to hold back the tears. After I hung up the phone I wrote "Dylan" for him.Shortly after the service I had to move out of my apartment, I was going through some old boxes when I found a few poems I wrote when I was in school back when I was fourteen years old. "Shelby", "Grandpa". "Time", "Rose" and "Fire" I wrote when I was eighteen. I hope you enjoy all of these.

Dylan

Lost in the night
Is a child
More innocent and beautiful than the stars
Our thoughts of him will always be with us
In mind and in heart
Though the pain of our loss pulses within us
We know that he is safe
We will always remember our smiling sweetheart

Time

Time is something we take for granted
It has no place, nor person
It's what we live for
Loss of innocence
Loss of youth
All come with time
The next time you have a minute
To yourself
Take it
Sit back relax and enjoy it
It may be your last

Shelby

Looking in her innocent face wondering
What's going through her mind?
A baby
So sweet and precious
With years of learning and experience ahead of her
Wishing I could shelter her from pain
And lead her to success
Only she must learn and develop on her own
Hoping she makes the right choices
With the right guidance
And if not
I'll love her the same

Grandpa

There are no words that can express how much I
love you and how much you mean to me,
From the fun in the garden, to my first sting from a bumble bee.
You've always been there no matter how long the haul,
When I'd watch you shave and you'd tuck me in before night would fall
You always made me laugh through think and through thin,
You always cheered me on even if I didn't win.
From your soft gentle hands and beautiful white hair,
You just knew how to show that you care.
Though parting with you is hard and tough,
Letting you know I'll always love you must be enough

Rose

Gently falling to the ground
Not even making a single sound
With a smell as sweet as honey
You could never have enough money
To buy the meaning of a rose
It's a symbol everyone knows
All about love, as strong as it can be
You have to feel it in order to see
The beauty that it may hold
Cannot be bought or sold

Fire

Hot coals taunting you
Large flames dazzling you
Dancing embers soaring up into the sky
Gliding like lightening bugs
Hot flaring caves sparkling like rubies
It pulls you in with warmth and fascination
Too hot to touch
But, too intense to look away

Encouragement

My earlier work is a little juvenile but it is a part of my growth as a writer which I am proud of even though I am my own worst critic. I had an English teacher in high school that was very influential on my direction as well as the inspiration to write. He noticed a talent in me almost as soon as I started his class and he would often challenge me with extra writing projects. Mr. Mc C was an eccentric, funny teacher with a passion for drama of the theatrical nature. There was one time when we were reading Julius Caesar. When we all arrived at the portable (which was our class room) he was standing on the railing. "Don't come any closer or I will jump!" of course we all looked at him like he was crazy. So he jumped, very dramatically I might add, it made the whole class laugh and we all seemed to have a little more interest that day. I can thank him for my love of Shakespeare to this day. Since Mr Mc C often challenged me with extra credit writing projects, I really think that he helped set the tone for my passion for poetry. This one day he pointed at a picture in the classroom entitled "Lady Shallotte" he asked me if I could write about how the picture made me feel "What do you see Belle?" I hope you enjoy what I created...

I think my "Dark Prince" would fit in after "Lady Shallotte" because it is a descriptive short story as well, though it was not inspired by anything other than my love of vampires and Anne Rice. I have always loved when I read any of her books, how it made me feel like I was there too. I could see it all in my head and felt like I was part of the story. My next project I am working on is a novel and I hope it is as enjoyable as I think this book is starting to be.

Lady Shallotte

Finally at ease she sat in an old wood boat, with tears running down her face. Lady Shallotte gazed into the cool, refreshing, green water as the misty breeze dosed the three, white candles simultaneously. For she had a desperate, striking pain in her breast, all she ever loved was snatched away in a millisecond. She felt as if every last piece of her weak and frail heart had been jumped on repeatedly. She and Phillip had been sworn to eternal everlasting love, and it was now all gone for his innocent soul was stolen. Her long, flowing, white linen dress dragged in the pond, sopping up the cool, fresh water. The boat seemed to float so gently across the rippling water through the lily pads, bull rushes and tall grass. Nothing about this faintly odd afternoon affected her, for she tossed through the pictures and memories in her head, longing to be able to climb in and enjoy them one last time.

Dark prince

There he lies in his dark, vacant coffin. Cursed with skin, untouched by light and a heart untouched by love. His mind is darkened or maybe taken over by evil and vicious thoughts of tasting blood and giving pain. Power is something he does not lack so watch your thoughts when he is near for he can read and see through you at anytime. He suddenly pushes aside the large stone lid of his coffin and emerges from the musty lair in which he dwells until dusk arrives. Now it is here and a violent churning hunger pulses within him, he must venture out into the night.

He lurks in the shadows and dark alleys patiently waiting for someone to draw near. Oh wait..... What is this?... a young girl, walking home.... alone?? He can feel his hunger grow stronger, as she doddles casually down the alley humming a quaint little tune. He can smell her perfume as he lingers, ready at any time to pounce like a cat attacking its prey. For she is the prey, he waits, already able to taste her blood on his tongue. Then out of the shadows he lunges, snatching her up and splicing her pail tender skin. He has his fill and unremorsefully he tosses her frail, lifeless body to the ground. Leaving her with nothing but death and two puncture wounds on her neck. In seconds he is gone to quest onward so that he may hunt his next victim.

Infatuation

Well where do I take you next? Oh I know, I had this guy friend that I had a crush on but he didn't look at me that way it was pretty obvious to him but not entirely to me. At the same time I had this other guy friend that worshiped the ground I walked on, it was very plain to see that he liked me a lot but I didn't feel the same way which I thought he knew. We were great friends, we hung out all the time. He made me laugh and we would cruise around in his little white dodge colt smoking pot and writing poetry. He was the only person that could talk more and faster than I could which is why I called him Natter Chatter that with the fact his last name was Natrasony. Which for some reason I could never remember. So he really liked me but I really liked the other guy even though Natter Chatter and I were so close. This next poem "The Heart Stealer" was inspired by this silly little love triangle.

The heart stealer

There is a guy who fancies me
I think he'd be better with my friend you see
He has a brain and can think with it too
Only thing is I'd rather be with you
He takes me out and treats me good
He sits and listens like I wish you would
If I let him take me in his arms and hold me tight
He would probably want me to stay every night
I know you don't love me and can't find it inside
The feelings I have are too strong, I cannot hide
So I carry on with my book and my pen
Maybe one day if I see you again
I hope we'll run away and fulfil our goals
Then you'll replace my heart that a long time ago you stole
I know in my life, how things go, it'll never work
So I'm writing this to tell you I don't think you're a jerk
Also if one day you ever need someone to hold you
I know in my heart to you, I would always be true

Sexuality

So I have loved and lost and loved again, we all go through it. It's a part of finding "The one" that special person that makes your heart skip a beat. So many times I swore I would never love again or said I was going to change teams because a woman would never hurt me the way a man has. All that aside, with every heart break I learned something new. At the very least I learned what I didn't want in a man. At times I learned I needed to care less and give them space or that I needed to care more and tell him everything I was doing. In the end, I learned to be myself and be true to myself. I try not to be too dramatic and always give a man his space when he needs it. I truly believe there is someone out there for all of us, just remember if you stay in an unhealthy relationship, he or she might pass you by and you won't even know it. Don't tie yourself down to someone who hurts you or makes you feel like less of a person. You are beautiful and I don't even know you but, I know you are. The only person worth your time is the one that sees that and lets you know every day. Love is an amazing thing, if you find it, it can help you endure your most intense challenges. I have written many poems inspired by love that was great and by love that was absolutely terrible but, I have always learned from that love. Trust me, there were times I thought I would never be able to carry on or even pick myself up off the floor. Sometimes I stayed in bed for days crying but, that never made me feel better. Life can pass you by if you shut yourself in and give up. I would write about it and try to let it go, some were easier than others but, I always moved on. I have grown used to people I love leaving or excepting the ones I wish would love me but could not. This made me realize I should leave the toxic environment. This next section of poems are inspired by love lost, love gained and just love whether or not it was good or bad. I know you probably wish I would get into the details but, that would be too personal...

Whole heart

To you I give my whole heart
Nothing more or nothing less
In hopes we'll have a new start
Since you've been gone I've been a mess
I love you more than I can explain
I pray each night you'll love me too
For when I'm with you I don't feel plain
I know that I'll never be blue
This of course is a fairy tale
That I had once before
I'll try not to let my dreams go stale
It's hard to be strong you're not here anymore
For now I'll think of you as my hero
You'll save my day and love me true
Romance that chases away my sorrow
So to leave my whole heart for you

Sacred Love

Touch me silent in the darkness
Tickle me sweet with your tongue
Hold me closely as if I'm precious
Then you'll know our sacred love has begun

Sing out loud like you were naked
Shed a tear but, you don't mourn
Don't fill your heart with lots of hatred
In my arms you are reborn

Hold my ballad in your breast
Don't let it escape through your lips
I will try you like the best
As you gently grasp my hips

We'll indulge in each other forever
Till day light comes no more
If you leave my heart will sever
Cause when you left it tore

Angel

Captivated by sexual thoughts
I breathe deeply, hoping to control my erotic desires
One look into his deep lustful eyes and a grasp
Of his powerful embrace,
I cannot master my fantasies
I am dominated by my longing
For his gentle touch and passionate kisses
The feeling of complete self-worth
So strong I feel that I could spread my wings and fly
For I am an angel

Now or never

You lay beside me with your hand on my waist
I took a deep breath then looked you in the face
With lips as soft as down feathers
You took my head in your hands and kissed me so tender
I let my fingers caress your chest
Feeling the creases of rippling muscles and nicely formed pecks
Your touch is so gentle it makes me quiver
It makes me want you to hold and touch me for ever
You lifted my leg and ran your hand inside my thigh
I whispered words of ecstasy and with those I do not lie
I told you what I'd like to do to you and where I could take you
You grasped me in your bulging arms and
told me what you'd put me through
I said, I didn't care "hush, and take me now"
For what the future brings we know not when or how
I want to feel your body held so close to mine
So that I can savour and enjoy you like a bottle of expensive white wine
If you fulfil my fantasies with me you will stay
Because a new erotic adventure will happen everyday

The wave

As the wind blew through my hair.
The breeze whispered sweet, soft thoughts of such tender, sexy words.
Romance I wish I could grasp in the palm of my hand.
For to love is to embrace each other, feeling the warmth
and passion tingling through your bodies.
Two naked figures drowning in lust, enjoying it to the fullest.
My thought or maybe 'dream' was swept away and lost as a wave
crashes against the shore then becomes one with the ocean once again.

Perpetually sad

We went to the beach and
Walked in the sand
He said I was beautiful as
I was holding his hand
We laid on the dock and looked
Up at the stars
I can tell you right now this
Mans not from mars
He kissed me gently and
Held me tight
I stayed in his arms for the
Whole night
He was big and strong and
As smart as can be
The only thing was
He couldn't stay with me
He lives far away
And must return home

So all I have now
Is this special poem
Why must it always
Turn out like this
I just want a guy
I can love, hold and kiss
Without having to worry
That he'll go away
Instead only with me
Forever he would stay
Although that's not how it works
Otherwise I'd be glad
I know I'm destined
To be perpetually sad

Sista

Black nights lit with white light,
Two friends torn from spite.
Light a candle and say a prayer,
She'll hear your thoughts and feel you there.
It's not because a lover is lost,
Just sad how much a friendship can cost.
Don't take my heart and lead me astray,
The love of two friends will always pay.
My wish to you is you won't feel that pain,
I know from it myself there's nothing to gain.
So I'll blow out our candle with love in my heart,
What we have I hope will never part.

Unsure

I find myself going in circles
Not knowing what I want
Someone light spirited and care free
Or laid back with two feet on the ground

My fear of real serious commitment
Drives me away from the earth drawn type
But the airborne ones make me afraid
Scared of love lost again

I don't want a broken heart
Yet I fear for it being captured
I want to fly with the eagles
And run with the horses

I think if I sit and wait
What I'm looking for will find me
But I'm tired of being alone
I need someone I can love

My dream lover

My dream lover would be willing to share my dreams and emotions
Feel my feelings, fulfill my desires
I want to tell him my fantasies and goals without criticism
Someone that will love me for what's in my head and my heart
Not just for my face and body
He has to want me for who I am not what I am
I want to laugh and have fun with him
But, if I need a shoulder to cry on and
someone to listen and understand
He is there and I will be there for him too
We will find that we can talk about anything and still get along
Because we listen to each other's views not trying to change them
He'll accept me the way I am and we'll grow and experience together
If he treats me good I'll treat him better
I want to feel the passion and electricity radiating through us
When we go to sleep and wake up in the morning together
He takes me places I've never been before
without even leaving the house
Through the good or bad, rain or shine he'll be
willing to keep trying and never give up
Sadly each morning I must wake up from my
dream and join reality once again

Wishing

I roll over and watch you sleep
As the morning sun peeks through my bedroom
curtains and warms your gentle face
Just to see you lying there
So peaceful and quiet in your deep slumber
I reach out to touch your cheek
Just feeling you next to me gives me such
comfort and security it puts me at ease
How I long to spend each day with you and
wake up next to you each morning
Knowing you love me and I love you
Without you, I am lost in a tornado of sorrowful emotions
But with you, each day is like a new adventure
You take a deep breath inhaling the love that clouds around you
Like the misty dew clouds on an April morn
I whisper "I love you" then snuggle up and fall back to sleep

Art

You hold my hand and
Run your fingers through my hair
We lay in the sand
In the distance I stare
I'm dreaming of love and
How it makes me feel
I can fly like a dove
Who says what's real
When you're floating in a daze
Way up in the sky
Life's just a maze
I'd rather soar high
In a land that's unknown
Unless you desire
For what's inside to be shown
Not strung on a wire
So show me true love
I'll give you my heart
We'll rise up above
Because sex is an art

All I can keep from this

I turn my back so you don't see my pain,
As much as I try to hide it
I care so much for you
So many things you did drove me crazy
But that's not what I'm thinking of now
You thought I wanted to be your girlfriend
But you were wrong
I just wanted you to love being around me
I didn't want you to love me
Just admitting I was special
Would have made me feel worth
A lot more than I feel right now
You showed me someone I thought
Was the most sensitive, caring man
I had met in a long time, but
You didn't want to be that person
Just pretend you were
There are so many good qualities you have
That you could go far and maybe
Make someone very happy one day
You made me happy for a little while
I thank you for that
I just wish it didn't have to be followed
By the sadness I feel

I'm not mad at you for not wanting to be with me
I just wish you went about it in a nicer fashion
So that I didn't feel so used and low
The times we spent together I will never forget
When I look back at them I will smile
Knowing that we had fun once
Hopefully one day you will be able to be my friend
With no resentment because I have already come to terms with things
By writing this here letter for you
The only thing I can keep from this is
A little spot in my heart reserved for memories of you

Innocence

I went through many ups and downs for a while but, I had an amazing job, great friends and a zest for life. I am going to give you some random poems now. When I come back things soon will start to get a little more serious, a time when I needed myself more than I could have ever imagined. So let me leave you with a few light hearted and fun poems before I get too deep and then transition into a sad time of my life.

I hope it doesn't rain

Walking in an endless space
Searching for the light
So I can feel the warmth on my face
Only till the night
If it comes back again tomorrow
I'll be happy all day
I will feel a great big sorrow
If it goes away
So on my quest I go again
I guess I run on solar power
That's why I hope it doesn't rain
If it does, I hate to say
I will turn quite sour

Life

We all have experiences that make us who we are
Sometimes their bad and leave us with a scar
Everyone grows and eventually matures
Then we must make decisions changing our futures
You can give it your all and go right to the top
Or not care one bit and let life come to a stop
It's all up to you; destiny is in your hand
Where it will take you, relies on what you demand
Don't shut the door on life and take what you've got
Venture, explore, and take in a whole lot
We only live once, so enjoy it while you're here
Do what you want, don't give into fear
When you die you'll know you had fun
If everything you wanted to do has been done

So much to say

I have so much to say
I don't know where to start
Walk on me if you may
I'll only take it to heart

You give out all you've got
Get nothing in return
Just because you care a lot
Even though, fires only burn

I've learned this lesson before
I don't think it'll be the same
I can't take anymore
Who is there to blame?

I guess my book is written
While still writing itself
When you read it I hope you're smitten
Please don't leave it on a shelf

Inspiration

Hello again! I love you if you are still here for this ride. If you haven't figured it out yet, or haven't read the prologue I have taken all these poems I wrote and the ones I like enough to bring on my journey and put in this book. At the end I have started at the beginning once again. If you don't understand it took me twenty-two years to write this book of poems. So now that I am done I am going back to the start of them all and reading them and taking you on my trip down memory lane as I recollect what happened or how I was feeling when I wrote them. This is quite the trip and I hope you enjoy the ride! It is interesting all the emotions this is stirring up. If I were to tell you my whole life story this book would be far too long and far too sad…. That is something I will write when I am old and my kids have children of their own. Considering all I have gone through, it is amazing I am as positive as I am. The thing is, tomorrow is a new day and if I spend my life dwelling on all the things that have gone wrong I would just waste my life. Far too many good people get lost that way. Instead, I learn something from my troubles and try to keep it from happening again. I have so much to be happy for; I have a roof over my head, food in my belly (maybe too much sometimes LOL) and a family that loves me. I have taught my children that no matter how rough of a day you might be having there is always someone out there whose day is much worse. I always look for good in everyday and everyone. Unfortunately, some people take a little deeper of a look than others. So here we are, on this trip through my memories that I get from all these poems I wrote in a little more than two decades of my life. Every extreme emotion, broken heart or empowering moment might be a little more bad than good but, it is me and how I dealt with it all! Now it's how I remember it! Many times in my life I have used my writing to help someone feel better about themselves or understand how I feel about them. These are a few of those.

A letter to my mother

Words cannot express how much I love you and how much you mean to me. I will try my hardest to show you now. The things you have been through to keep me safe and the discipline I needed to make me a good person. I thank you for, because it always showed how much you love me. As many times as I didn't show it I love you for each and everything you taught me. I will love you for everything I can learn from you in my years to come. You have been an inspiration for me to lead a good life and a perfect example of who I would like to be. I owe everything I am and everything I have today to your love and guidance. I hope one day I will be able to pass it all on to my children. Thank you for being the best mom anyone could ever ask for.

(Sadly I wrote this in hopes that she may have opened her heart. Unfortunately, it was like I never wrote it. I should have wrote the truth then I would have deserved the reaction I got)

A letter of encouragement

Sunday was an amazing day and I owe it all to an amazing guy "you" it's unbelievable how sincere you are. I must say your passion to enjoy life inspires me and your generosity astounds me. I had so much fun and was so relaxed it was exactly what I needed. You have restored my faith in men and I feel I can trust you. (This is a rare trait in most men) I hope you feel you can trust me too, because I would never tell anyone anything you ever told me. My one wish is that you will remind yourself every day that you are a wonderful person and you only deserve the best in life. If the one you care for can't make you feel like you're as special as a moment of silence or as beautiful as a sunset then you know they don't love you enough. You are the only person you have to live with for the rest of your life so you have to like yourself. Here's an old saying I like to finish my letter "If you want to fuck with the eagles you got to learn how to fly!" I have faith that you will fly!

Torment

The next portion of this book is going to go to a dark place for a while and I hope I don't scare you off. I ended up falling in love with someone who was bad for me. Yes, I left that misery with two beautiful children but it took a lot of tears, broken bones and bruises to survive it and there were times I didn't think I could go on any longer but I always did. I am a fighter and I had two amazing reasons to keep fighting. So I may not explain it all and there will poems that don't seem so bad but this was the saddest and darkest part of my life. Yet at the same time it was the most gorgeous part because it was when my children were born. Which made it so bitter sweet, I guess that is why this is the hardest part to remember....

Tink

In the magical world of Disney
There is always a happy ending
A wishing star or a fairy godmother
Here in our world
Things don't always happen that way
If I had my way it would all be perfect
I hope you get your happy ending one day
Maybe you'll find your wishing star
To light the way back
To the fairy you loved once upon a time

Trapped

In a maze of dead ends
I struggle
To find a way
Any way
To get out
The illusion of being free
Can become a reality
But, it takes time
Only the person
Who is trapped in the maze
Can find the strength
In their selves
To break through the dead ends
And then
Only then
Can be free

Bereft

I struggle not to feel the pain
The one I once loved has left
All my emotions I try to strain
So I must not feel bereft
He magically danced into my life
Making the flowers bloom just for me
Not to get caught in his love I strife
If I could open my eyes and really see
The world that's around me is painted pink
Though I know this is not reality
My brain is fogged and I cannot think
I'm afraid of losing my sanity
For he is a man who will break my heart
Yet in his arms forever, I wish to be
I should have known this of him from the start
Yet I hope for my love to come back to me
(Sometimes the best lessons learned are the hard ones)

Candy coating

Look at you, another one of THEM
The not so dying breed of CHARMERS
I had a feeling that was so deep, I thought it was real
You seemed not to be like the OTHERS
But once you crack the candy shell. . ...
I see. . ...
There is NO chocolate within. . ...

Jerk

I held your hand
I was your friend
I did not demand
My wounds will mend
I tried my best
I thought we'd work
You're like the rest
A fucking jerk
I gave you a chance
And a couple more
We used to dance
Now I'm just sore
So give me up
And turn away
You're like a pup
That's gone astray

Help (Addiction)

A horrible cycle of selfishness and greed
The anger and hostility all for a need
Not quite a necessity only a want
I guess because your days and dreams it does haunt
Strips you of all of your happiness in life
Like it actually slices your heart with a knife
Leaves you with an empty soul and tired mind
It won't help you look for something you can't find
So if you want a way out then please take my hand
I'll lead you to a place where we all understand

Hollow

The one I want
Can't love me for me
My heart he does taunt
I wish he could see
I try to show him my love
And how much that I care
It's as beautiful as a dove
That you must not scare
For if she flies away
She might not return
If you're gentle she'll stay
This you must learn
The first step is trust
The rest will follow
Especially the lust
So your heart won't be hollow

Humans

Constant confusion
Unexplainable tension
I pull out my hair
I gnash my teeth
All in the name of love
For what reason must we endure this?
Our own punishment
For the lustful pleasure of another's embrace
Like animals we survive
Like kings we live
And like children we fight

Word of advice

I've been told once or twice
This word of advice
That I'm giving to you
I hope you get the clue
Don't ever trust a man
Avoid them if you can
They'll take you for a ride
And make sure they cover their hide
Then they run away
To return another day
To break your heart again
I'd rather deal with rain
Then shed another tear
The pain is what I fear
I'm glad I left you this letter
You won't think it'll get better
Then you'll light a smoke
And get rid of that joke
Break your heart? Never!
Now he's gone forever!

Admiration

In the midst of this hell I was living through I had a friend that was like a white light. She taught me how important life was and that I needed to fight for it! Fight for freedom from this jail cell of abuse. Her name was Katrina. When we met she was dating a great guy with a lot of health problems. He was sweet and loved her so much. Shortly after their love story began she was diagnosed with a rare form of cancer and she was terminal. At eighteen years old when her life was just getting started she had to come to terms with the fact that she was going to die. Katrina was an amazingly strong, smart, loving and fun girl; she had the biggest heart and an infectious laugh. There were times that if she hadn't lost all her hair from the chemotherapy you would never even realize that she was sick. When we were together the time would fly by because we were always having so much fun. Katrina loved Russell so much and she finally got her dream to come true. They were married on Friday December 13/2002. It broke my heart not to be there but my ex felt threatened by our friendship because Katrina wanted me to leave him. She knew about the abuse and she wanted more for me. She wanted me to be happy with someone that would truly love me the way I deserved. So he would not let me go to the wedding and I took a horrible beating that day for trying to go. She understood that I wanted to be there more than anything and it broke her heart to see me so badly bruised. She made me promise that I wouldn't spend the rest of my life putting up with this abuse because he would never change and if he wasn't willing to get help then I deserved better. Sadly, Katrina got sick quite quickly after her and Russell got married, it was already hard to handle not being able to see her everyday like I was used to but, knowing her time was drawing near was even harder. One night while I was at home missing the fun we had I wrote her a poem and when I got a chance to sneak out and go see her at the hospital I brought it to her. She was so happy to see my son and I and despite how sick she was it was a beautiful visit. My son had recently taken a few steps on his own (he was only ten months old at the time) and I had hoped he would take a few steps for Katrina since she loved him so much. I held him so that he was standing on the hospital floor and Katrina encouraged him to come to her and to our surprise he walked right to her. It was the first time he had walked all by himself and it was to her! To see the joy on her face when he did is something I will never forget. Before we left the hospital Katrina gave me her book of poetry and I promised if I had ever got my poems published that I would put a few of her's in my book and I will not break that promise. Later that night after I had gone to sleep I heard the phone ringing, it was Katrina's sister Tanya, she had called to tell me that Katrina was gone. I had a hard time dealing with it because I had never lost someone I loved that was that young with so much more life to live. Russell passed away several years later and I think they are both at rest together. If there is anything I learned from them both, it is not to take life for granted. We only get one life and we need to enjoy each and every bit of it! So before I go back to more of the chaos I was going through with my ex I will share a little bit of the talent Katrina had as well as the poems I wrote for her and Russell.

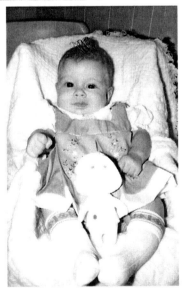

Something's wrong

On a journey
But still at home
With the family
But all alone

In my own little world
No one around
It's so quiet
Yet, noise surrounds

Away from the world
In a wide open space
I walk slowly
At a quick pace

Not saying a word
I sing a song
I don't know what
But something's wrong

Written beautifully by
Katrina Mae-Shaw

Pointless

As a bird
With no wings
And a weight on its feet

As a deer
That's been shot
And keeps a heart beat

As a flower
With no food
Water nor sunlight

As a little one
That's picked on
And unable to fight

So is the life
Without any friends
It's pointless
Why not let it end?

Written beautifully by
Katrina Mae-Shaw

Momentary death

When you die
Your body lies
In your wooden coffin bed

Away from crime
To a world with no time
A beginning but no end

Nothing to fear
For you're no longer here
No worries, no pain, no sorrow

No more laughter
No more joy
No today and no tomorrow

So when you die
And your body lies
In your wooden coffin bed

Think of your friends
That you'll meet again
In the promised world ahead

Written beautifully by
Katrina Mae-Shaw

I hate you

I hate the way you smile
And the stubble on your chin
I hate the way my eyes light up
Whenever you walk in

I hate the way you read my mind
And the way that you would stare
I hate the way you said "I love you"
As you ran your fingers through my hair

I hate the way you hugged me
And said I was the only one
I hated it when we'd sit and talk
Of everything under the sun

I hate the way I despise
Everything you do
Because you love someone else
As much as I love you

Written beautifully by
Katrina Mae-Shaw

88

Katrina Mae

How do I tell you I love you dear friend
Without having to say that we're nearing the end
Of a beautiful friendship filled with love and laughter
That I wish could go on forever and after
You've told me your secrets and I told you mine
If I we're to say I won't miss you I would be lying
I will always have you in my mind and my heart
This isn't an ending; it's a brand new start
To what you deserve for being who you are
Just remember your utopia isn't very far

In loving memory of Katrina Mae-Shaw
Feb 25, 1983- Jan 26, 2003

Russell & Katrina

I see the morning sun kissing
The dew with a glisten so brilliant
The wind tries to compete
With a graceful south breeze
A feather takes to the air
Spinning and dancing
Suddenly a delicate butterfly
Stretches her wings and decides to chase
An elliptical dance begins
An aura so captivating so magical
Life is a dance and sometimes
When we find the right person
We always know the steps and keep the beat
There are very few in life who find love
True love
If you find the love of your life
You will put on those shoes and
Dance right to heaven
I know that Russell and Katrina are there
Dancing all over heaven
May they always be in our hearts
Dancing with the angels

Affliction

I thought a lot after Katrina passed and watching how sad and broken hearted Russell was really made me realize that I just didn't feel that strong for the one who beats me. I finally got the guts up to ask him to leave and I had a little help from a few of my friends as well as my cousin, they would stay with me so I wasn't alone. It worked for a while but, eventually people have lives and can't always be there so he finally sucked me in to the black hole again. Shortly after I found out that I was pregnant with my daughter so I thought I would give it one more honest try. Not long after my beautiful little girl was born things got bad again. I found this awesome little cabin on the water out south of town, it was so private I figured he would never find me out there. Unfortunately he had been sleeping with my best friend for months and she told him where I had moved. I never could figure out who told him, I never thought it would have been her. Once he found me out there it was over for me. The beatings got worse and far more often since there was nobody close enough to hear me scream and cry for my life. It was getting to the point where I was ready to give up. We were in and out of the local safe house and I would charge him with assault but a restraining order is only a piece of paper and it did not protect me....

What will become of me

What will become of me?
Where will I go?
Will I run to the sea?
No one will ever know
I won't have a roof over our heads
Or a place to hang my hat
No where to put our beds
How did it end up like that?
I don't want to be sent away
To somewhere I do not know
So I guess I'll have to pray
So that you can watch the kids grow
Will my dreams ever come true?
Or be washed away by tears
I need to be close to you
Not alone to face my fears
So I guess I'll see tomorrow
If I can still hold you tight
I'm already filled with sorrow
I can't bare another lonely night

Missing you

I know it's hard when we're so far away
to remember all the things we want to say
To have a moment to spend with me
If there was only a way we could make them see
Just how in love we are and how much you care
You are my soul mate, to keep us apart isn't fair
just to be with you and feel your embrace
They got you jumping through hoops like it's a race
I hope for the day, this will be over and done
We'll be happy and they'll know that we've won
I'll love you forever not even in death will we part
Without you in my arms, I'll never have a whole heart

Empty

I feel empty yet filled
With sorrow
Though I will make it
To see tomorrow
My journey is laid out
Before me
But a lonely trail is
All I can see
My heart is longing to be
With you
On a beautiful beach just
Us two
That just seems so
Far away
I need to live my life
For each new day
All I can say
Is stay the course
I will be here
For better or worse
A lonely heart
Waiting for its soul
With you back in my arms
So I can feel whole

Hopeless desperation

The funny thing is that I am caught up in my own self realization
This hopeless desperation
For a rational thought that synchronizes with my
hopes and aspects for what I may become
The inevitable battle that fights my every will
The continuous thought of how we'll pay our bills
To conclude our next suffice
Sure hope it ends off nice
I will take another chance
Just to take a kick in the pants

First star

On one moonlit night
I saw the first star
It was a beautiful sight
Although it seemed so far

I sat in a daze
Then my wish I sent out
My mind in a haze
I started to shout

Did you hear my request?
I made it quite clear
Now you do the rest
Or I'll shed another tear

Bring me my man
With a heart of gold
Make him wise if you can
Just not too old

Here to stay

Slipping under the mat
Being swept aside
I don't know where I'm at
I just want to cry
Things can change so fast
Like a winters day
When you think the sun will last
It seems to run away
I need to hold you tight
Even just to watch you play
To kiss your eyes goodnight
Once you're finally here to stay

Darkness

At the top of a mountain
How can you fall in the landslide again?
You saw it coming
You've slid farther before
With every step you slid
How could you walk that trail again?
So dark and gloomy full of shadows
What were you thinking?
What did you want?
What else could you expect?
Other than darkness

Don't kick the dog

I have spent my life trying
To figure things out
Yet I am still so puzzled
With myself
It's as if I get it all figured out
And then I just have to
Fuck myself over
Like picking up the dog
After you kick him and
Then kick him again
An unbelievable premeditation
Of destruction

Chance & Devin

Your innocence is captivating
As the dreams dance around in your head
So comfortable in your peaceful slumber
Such delicate features like baby angels
I wish you could stay this small forever
One day you'll grow and leave the nest
Like a bird that learns to fly
I hope you soar high above the clouds
Just remember to bring back a piece of heaven for mom
Like the piece I had all the years
That you were my babies

Love Mom

For the last time

It's hard sometimes to see you
And hold back what I want to say
I hoped without my loving words
That you would find your way
You'd realize what I meant to you
And never want to lose me
Your heart no longer loves me
That I can now see
I thought we'd grow old together
With our two we brought to life
That I was your one and only and
One day would be your wife
I long to hold you close and
Feel you embrace me too
That will never happen now
So for that last time, I love you

Why

Why do I apologize?
When I look into your eyes
Just to hear some more lies
You wonder why I despise.
You're the one with the fist
While I'm here with my list
Of all the things that you missed
Hell yea I'm fucking pissed
You say I was wrong
You are the one who is strong
In a place you don't belong
Yet it took me so long
To see you for whom you are
Why do I get another scar?
My face you did mare
Why do you go so far?
I need to find a way out
While you stand here and shout
There is no need for you to pout
It's your story that I doubt
I deserve so much more
Then you running off with a whore
My head is so damn sore
And my dress that you tore
While I tried to get away
In hopes to live another day
Why did it end up this way?
Why the fuck do you stay?
Please just go away!

(Why would anyone ever beat the one they say they love?)

Enlightenment

My dear precious reader, I don't think you know how special you are to me. Looking back now is still so hard it seemed impossible when I went through it but I survived, barely but I did, I am still here. At the time I thought I knew what love was and I did truly love him and maybe he did love me, no matter how cruel and twisted he showed it. I think it is the only way he knew how. Even after having my face reconstructed I stayed, it wasn't until I came home from the doctor the day after a severe beating that my four year old son said "I am sorry mommy." "Why are you sorry baby?" I asked. He replied with the saddest little look on his face "If I don't jump on my bed my Daddy don't have nothing to hit you with." I said "No baby it's not your fault, anything he does is never your fault!" it was then I realized I had to get away for the sake of my children. I didn't want my son to become an abuser or my daughter to become a victim. So I put us in the local safe house for our longest stay. We had been there before but never this long. It took a mountain of strength to leave him but he would not just leave us alone. I could not get free of this man (If you could call him that). It wasn't until a bigger stronger but gentler man started to care for me and he was tired of watching the twinkle in my eyes slowly disappear. When we were in the safe house he noticed the twinkle start to come back and I would slowly start to be happy again but, as soon as I was on my own and my ex would force his way back in my life, it would disappear all over again. One day I called up that gentle giant and asked if he could come pick me up at the hospital, this last beating almost killed me and I was scared to be alone. I was afraid next time, because there was always a next time, he would be successful. On the drive from the hospital that sweet man asked me "Do you want to be with this guy? Do you want him in your life?" I replied "No, I just can't get rid of him!" so he packed us up and moved us out to his house. It didn't take long for me to see what love truly was, what it was like to feel safe and really loved. I was so badly beaten for so long though it took some time for me not to be on the defence all the time so there were some ups and downs between us. I had to learn that I was with someone who didn't want to hurt me, that only wanted to love me even if we don't agree about everything. So these next poems I wrote for him.

Thankful

Broken down, beaten, bleeding and bruised
Crying on the floor, feeling so used
Those days in my life are far behind me
Yet they left me with a scar only I can see
I begged for my life more times than I can remember
As he beat me with a steel pipe one cold November
Gasping for air, crawling across the lawn
Feeling as fragile as a baby fawn
Until a big strong man came to our rescue
To protect us and love us through and through
If he had not saved us I wouldn't be here
My ex would have killed me is what I fear
So I am thankful for my knight in shining armour
Who packed us up and moved us away so far

Finding myself

Finding who I am again a well travelled road but,
This time it's different
There is a soft aroma of peace with a faint essence of tranquility
The trees seem more graceful
The moss is lush and fuller beneath my feet
Quietly the wind circles me slowly
I see more beauty on my trail of life

Coming out of the shadows

Before you found me I was lingering in the shadows almost nonexistent, almost dead. I never thought I could reach a point so low that I could not look at myself, could not feel or even be aware of how quickly I could destroy myself. Like a wind storm whisking away all that was good, all that was happy. Till you were my anchor, holding me down through the largest gusts and keeping me grounded in a time when I would have let myself just blow away. You brought back the sun and pushed away the clouds. So that now I can feel the warmth on my face, breathe the fresh air and feel your love in my heart. With your big strong arms I can feel your embrace, I can feel safe. Sometimes I want to climb inside you and hide from the world but, instead you stand strong behind me so that I can face each new dilemma with pride and hold my head high. Why? Because I have someone who loves me even though you know my skeletons I left in the shadows and you only care about what we have in the light of each new day

The way you make me feel

The way you look at me makes my heart flutter
That dimple when you smile causes me to stutter
You're gentle and shy, I want to feel your touch
I haven't known you long but I like you so much

When I play with your hair it's as soft as down feathers
Oh! How you took my head in your hands and kissed me so tender
I thought men like you only existed in dreams
This is the passion I wanted and you too it seems

If you stay a while you'll see how much love I have inside
And I hope whatever feelings you have you won't hide
If I scare you at all please let me know
I'd rather that then have to see you go

Little things mean a lot

When we cuddle together and
You play with my hair
It's a simple little way
To show that you care
When dinner is done and
The table is clear
I'm washing the dishes say
Would you like a smoke dear
I'll clean the house and
Manage the bills
You'll work hard and
Hike lots of hills
I'll stand beside you till
Death do we part
Never be afraid
To show me your heart
When the world around me
Seems it won't stop
Just remind yourself
Little things mean a lot

I will try to always have socks and
Underwear clean
If some morning I forget
Please don't be mean
I'll roll your smokes and
Make you a lunch
Just think of my needs
There must be a bunch
If I look tired and
Something's in my head
Ask me what is wrong
Before you go to bed
All I know is when
Tempers get hot
Remind yourself
Little things mean a lot

Now that you're gone

I know you don't love me and can't find it inside
The feelings I have are too strong I cannot hide
So here I am sad and blue
When all I had to say was I love you
I know it's too late and things went wrong
I find I hurt more, now that you're gone
I'd walk the earth just to bring you back
With what you think now you won't give me slack
The things I like I can't do anymore
Doing them without you makes my heart sore
Just knowing I can't look in your eyes again
Always brings me so much pain
If I write it down as if it were a letter
I find it helps when I need to feel better

For the one I love

The day I knew
That this was love
Will live in my memory
For I couldn't believe
All this happiness
Was happening to me
I felt something in my heart
That was so true
I knew I waited all my life
To fall in love with you

How special you are

Passion that could build mountains
Lust that could move them
Is only the beginning of what
You do for me
Your warm bedroom eyes burrow
Deep in my soul
How I long for your gentle touch
Caressing my heart with tingly
Feelings of joy
You are the most beautiful thing
I have ever laid my eyes upon
Yet I don't know if someday
You will realize just
How amazingly special you are

My essence

All is spinning yet falling too
My mind is open but always swelling
I take my thoughts and
Sprinkle them on the paper
Like a dance of gold fairies
Always thinking of places where
The sky never ends and I can fly
I almost feel a mist
Of sensual pleasure frolic
Through my limbs and out to my fingertips
The gentle glide of the pen
Soothes my soul
Demons and hauntings
Trembling with fear for
What I might unfold in my book

Imagine

The way I feel when you are with me is so amazing
I can't help but get lost in your eyes
Now that you are not here I try not to get lost by sadness
Instead I think of you and smile
I think about how it makes me feel when you look at me
How it feels just to sit and watch you
If I close my eyes I can pretend you're here holding me
I can almost feel your sweet breath on my neck
I think of how I love touching you, holding you, loving you
I never thought you could feel so good from so far away
Every night before I fall asleep this is what I do
I dream you are there with me laughing and smiling
I guess you must be the man of my dreams
Because you are always in them

I think of you

With each breath I take I think of you
I wish to hold you close
To feel your embrace and smell your skin
Feeling your heart beating against mine
If only you were here not far away
I know you are there so that we can have
All the things we want and need
The only thing is all I want is you
You are the love of my life and best friend
They say that absence makes the heart grow stronger
I don't think my love for you
Could grow any bigger than it already is

Our love

Our love is so strong that each emotion is so
intense whether they are good or bad
I'd walk to the end of the earth for one good moment with you
To be completely connected to our inner souls
To be one being so enthralled by love
So inspired by each other that the world could pass us by and
We wouldn't even notice
There is nothing I would not do just to be with you

Thank you

If you listen careful and
Hear my thoughts
Take my hand when I am lost
Steal my pain when it almost kills me
You are my friend, you are my family
If you hold me close when I have fears
Comfort me when I shed tears
You make me know that I am loved
Pick me up when I've been shoved
You are my friend, you are my family
I appreciate you for all you've done
I love you more with each battle we've won
You're not just my friend, you are my family

The only friend

A blissful peace
My serenity
A feeling of security
A new knowledge of love
The flutter deep inside
That takes your breath away
With a breeze of enlightenment
A fire in my heart
That will always burn
As long as I have you
The only friend I need
Until forever is over

Whisper on the wind

I can smell your scent on my pillow as I lay my head down to sleep
I can hear your whisper on the wind as it blows through my hair
I can't feel you hold me when I dream I'm in your arms
I can't see your smile when I need to smile myself
I await the day when you are back here again
When I can feel the love you give me as I take
you in my arms and hold you close
I never want to have to let you go again but, sadly, I soon will

To you

How do you do that?
Make me feel this way
Take my eyes off you, I can't
Just to be in your arms each day
I don't think I really knew love
Not the way I feel with you
I'm floating with the angels above
Because my heart belongs to you

Two old souls

Sleep doesn't feel the same when I'm not in your arms
Food has no taste and life feels dead
There is nothing I want more than to feel your breath on my neck
Your hands on my breasts and your lips caressing mine
Our love is like a dance between two old souls
With a song that never ends
My life is your life
My love and your love and my heart is yours for all eternity

You

Even though the train is
Going by
I sit here and wonder
Why
I was so lucky my
Dreams came true
It all happened when
I fell in love with you

Devoted adoration

Being a mother has brought me more joy than anything else I have ever done in my life. Of course it takes patience and it has its moments but, there is no job I love more. Both my children are so unique in so many ways and I love watching them become exactly who they want to be. My son is growing up to be such a handsome, mature young man who knows how to respect women and has his head on his shoulders, he is already planning his future. He has so much ambition to get a good education and find a job that pays well and is something he will enjoy doing. They both have such big loving hearts willing to help anyone in need and they make me feel good about the job I am doing raising them. My daughter is so creative with a huge imagination and a zest for life, she reminds me of someone I know, they both do. She is gentle and loving and has a beautiful voice. I imagine her doing something like fashion design or working with children, maybe even a writer like me. Music is in her soul, she has always felt the beat and has amazing rhythm. I know that as long as I encourage them to follow their dreams and that they can do anything they put their minds to! (I know I am repeating myself) I will do everything in my power to help them succeed and grow to be the best version of themselves they can be, and then I have done my job as a mother.

My teenage boy

Why don't you realize how much you scare me?
With your crazy stunts and you're so carefree
My life would be over if I ever lost you
We all would be devastated and oh so blue
You are my first born and my only boy
I know you're young but, your life's not a toy
If anything ever happened I'd be ripped apart
A life without you would tear out my heart
I want to be understanding as well as fair
I just don't think you know how much I care
Please be safe wherever you roam
Promise me you will always make it home

My teenage girl

I always wanted a little girl
Just so scary in this crazy world
I look at your beauty with concern
There is so much you need to learn
I will be here to guide the way
Fill you with confidence every day
There will be times you think I'm unfair
Like that time you wanted to dye your hair
Trust me when I tell you I'm right
Even when you put up a fight
I love you more than you'll ever know
Nothing makes me more proud then watching you grow
I will be here every time you need me
Until one day you're ready to set free

The love of a mother

I have asked myself a million times how could a mother love a child so much when the child was her only one? Then take it away to give to her other two, the ones she had last, the ones she had with a man she still loves. Did that child become less hers? Did that child deserve to feel worthless? Maybe because her father chose to give the child the love that was taken away. Yet I never knew the answer, I never understood how a mother could love her child any less than the first day she laid her eyes upon that child. If there is anything I have learned from this it is to love both my children the same. The same as each other and the same as the first day I laid my eyes upon them. They will never know what it is like to want their mothers love more than anything, more than life itself. They will have every ounce I have to give from their first day until my last! For no matter how old they get they never stop needing the love of their mother.

Melancholy

This next part is very hard for me to write about since it is still so fresh. One of the good things that came out of all the violence was my relationship with his family. I became very close with two of his brothers one of them was like a brother to me and our daughters are like sisters more than cousins. Even my bestie and he were super close so that horrible day when she came through my door in tears will haunt me forever. Right away I asked her what was wrong and she said "I just heard a rumor, please tell me it's not true" "What?" I asked. "I was told Trav is dead and you are the only person who could find out if it's true or not!" my bestie sobbed. So I grabbed the phone as I tried to hold back the tears. I called the other brother and I could hear it in his voice from the moment he said "Hello?" "I heard something terrible about Trav. Please tell me it's not true!" I pleaded. "Belle he is gone" I could hear the sadness in his voice. I cried so hard I made some of the blood vessels in my face, under my eyes burst. Our whole family was rattled to the core but, at the same time it sure brought us all together. We don't take each other for granted anymore, even my children who are teenagers now tell each other "I love you" far more often. They tell me every day and I tell them as often as I think of it which is every chance I get! I know I will never get to hug Travy, my bro ever again but, I spoke to him the night before we lost him and one of the last things I got to tell him was that I was publishing my book. He was so happy for me, he was one of my biggest fans, so it was fitting to make sure he was in it. I will always love him and his two beautiful children and I will always be here for them. This next poem is for him and the one after it was a silly poem I wrote for my bestie that Trav liked, that is why I put them together...

Tray

This empty feeling deep inside
That will not go away
A sullen look I cannot hide
So in my heart you'll stay

I always thought I would have you near
When I needed a hug or a smile
The emptiness is what I fear
I know it will linger a long while

Two beautiful children filled with sorrow
With so much life they want to share
It's just so hard to face tomorrow
When I think how you won't be there

With each new day I still ask why?
How someone so special could be gone
I refuse to believe it or say goodbye
As much as I need to, to carry on

I just can't accept you're really gone
If just once more I could hear your voice
I think I'd be able to carry on
If I only had that choice

Bitches

You're my girl
I love you so much
We'll tackle the world
Then go for lunch
Men can't affect us
We know where it's at
Fuck you and the bus
Mr. Man and your tat
You'll have my back
I will have yours
Men have no tack
With all their roars
Suck it up boy
We're sisters for life
I'm not your toy
Definitely not your wife

Tranquility

Holy crap! I took a little time to scroll back and see what I have created for this book and I am kind of surprised… It's really coming together; don't get me wrong it has been a lot of work… Trust me! The thing is to see all I have been through, the black eyes, stupid lies and even the beautiful moments I can never replace. They are all here within these pages, it's almost too scary of a thing that anyone, absolutely anyone can take a look inside my head and my heart. Yet I am proud of this accomplishment despite the fact that I never thought I would look at it as a book. It's not just a bunch of rambling no one wants to hear. Instead I am seeing what I always wanted it to be, a nice book of poems that might reach out to someone, who needs a strong person to say it's ok! I have been through it or something close, you will survive. Focus on what is most important to you and remember you are in charge of your own destiny. You are the only person you have to live with for the rest of your life. You have to love and respect yourself in order to live with you. I know sometimes you don't want to hear it because it's not the first time you have been told but, maybe this time your hair stood on end or you really truly felt the same way I have. I found as long as I never let anything stop me from putting a smile on my face and looking for the way up or out I would keep on going. I learned a long time ago I can do anything I put my mind to and so can you! I have enjoyed this little journey we took together and I hope that maybe you are just a bit stronger or happier from it because I sure am! So the last poem I will leave you with is one I wrote a long time ago but, I really love and believe to this day…

I am me

I am not what I was
Nor what I long to be
I am not what I should be
I am me

I was irresponsible
I long to be beautiful
I should be perfect
I am me

I know I'm responsible
I wish I was beautiful
No one is perfect
I am me

CPSIA information can be obtained
at www.ICGtesting.com
Printed in the USA
LVOW08*0343081117
555265LV00005B/9/P